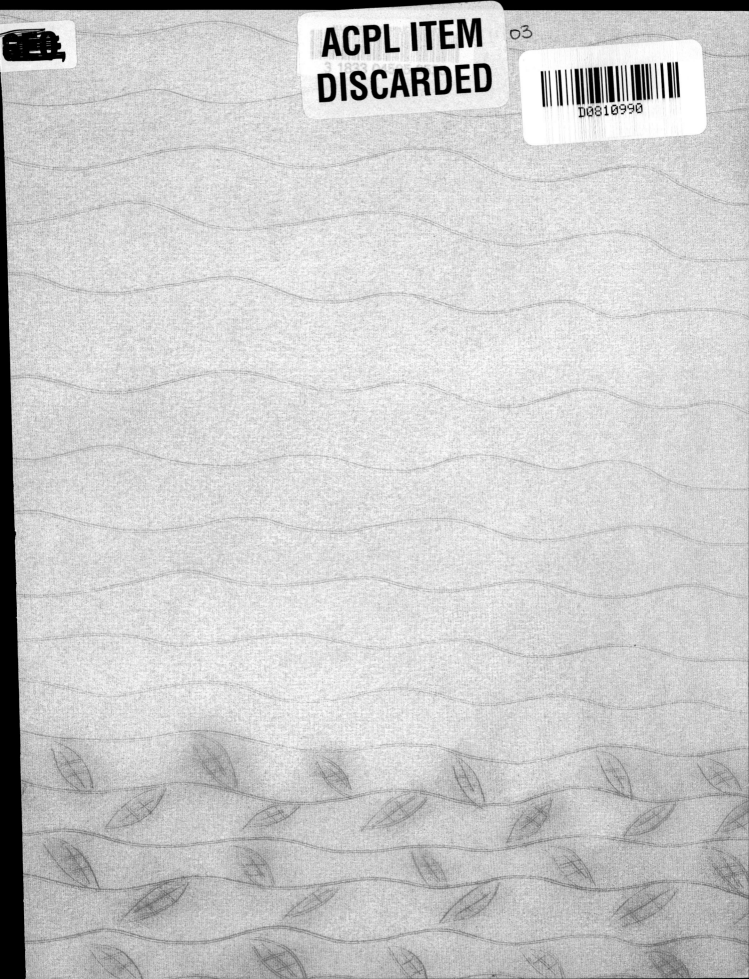

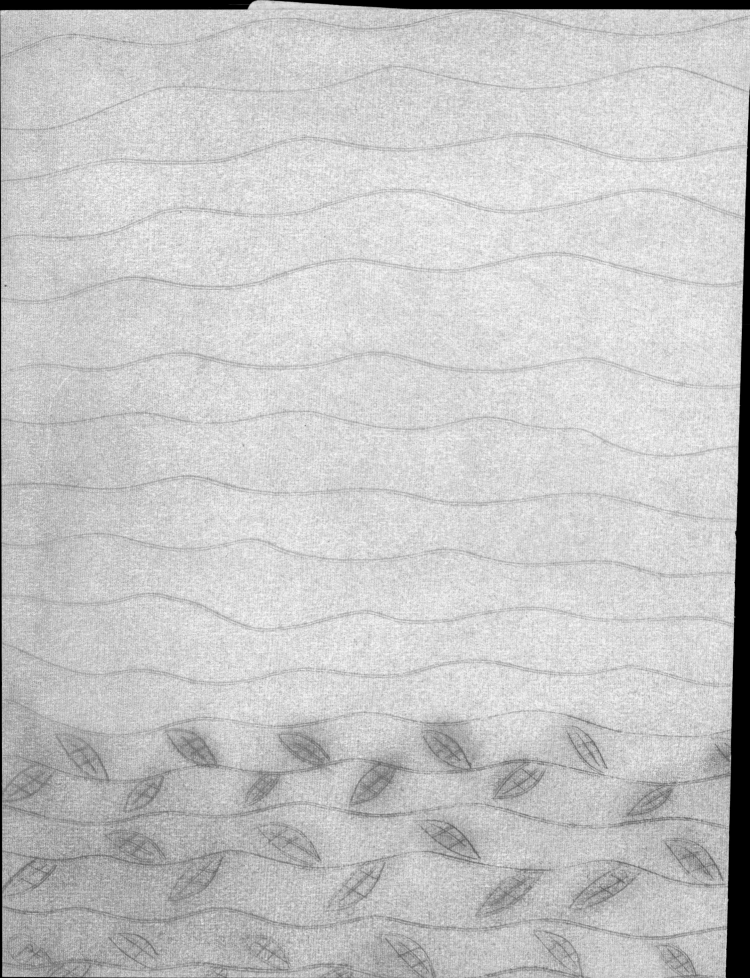

WILD WILD WORLD
MANTISES

by Liza Jacobs

BLACKBIRCH®
PRESS

THOMSON
★
GALE

San Diego • Detroit • New York • San Francisco • Cleveland • New Haven, Conn. • Waterville, Maine • London • Munich

Photographs © 1995 by Lee Wen-Kuei

Cover Photograph © Corel

© 1995 by Chin-Chin Publications Ltd.

No. 274-1, Sec.1 Ho-Ping E. Rd., Taipei, Taiwan, R.O.C.
Tel: 886-2-2363-3486 Fax: 886-2-2363-6081

LIBRARY OF CONGRESS CATALOGING-IN-PUBLICATION DATA

Jacobs, Liza.
  Mantises / by Liza Jacobs.
    v. cm. -- (Wild wild world)
Includes bibliographical references.
Contents: A mantis is an insect -- Meat-eaters -- Mating -- Dangers.
  ISBN 1-4103-0039-0
  1. Mantodea--Juvenile literature. [1. Praying mantises.] I. Title.
II. Series.

QL505.83.J23 2003
595.7'27--dc21
                                           2003001495

Table of Contents

A mantis has a long, thin body. Its triangle-shaped head can turn from side to side. It uses two thin antennae to feel and smell.

Like other insects, mantises have compound eyes. Compound eyes are made up of hundreds of tiny eyes. This gives mantises amazing eyesight. During the day, the eyes of a mantis look light green. At night, they become dark. This helps a mantis see at night.

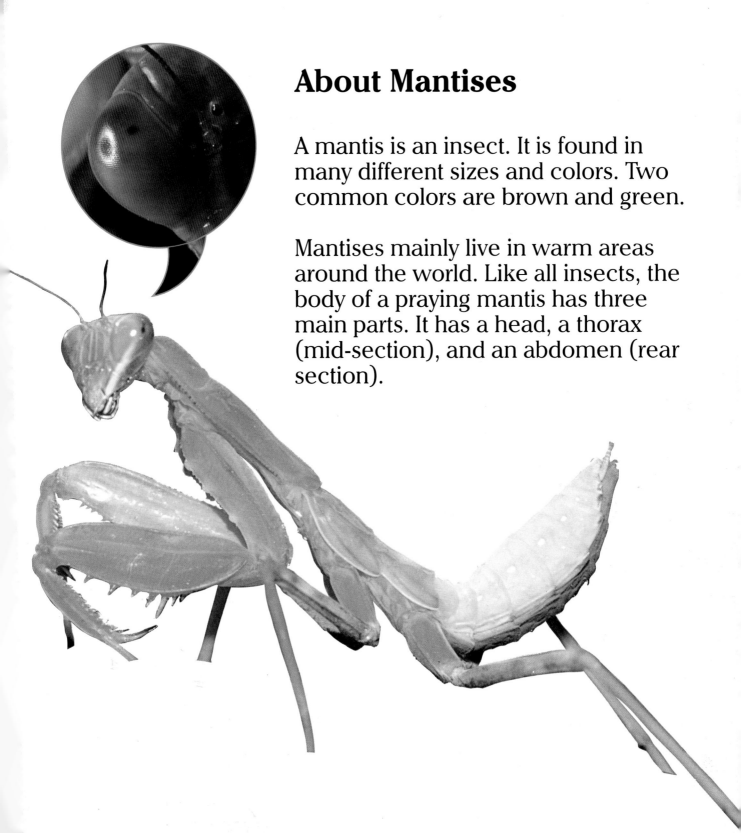

About Mantises

A mantis is an insect. It is found in many different sizes and colors. Two common colors are brown and green.

Mantises mainly live in warm areas around the world. Like all insects, the body of a praying mantis has three main parts. It has a head, a thorax (mid-section), and an abdomen (rear section).

Like all insects, it has three pairs of legs.

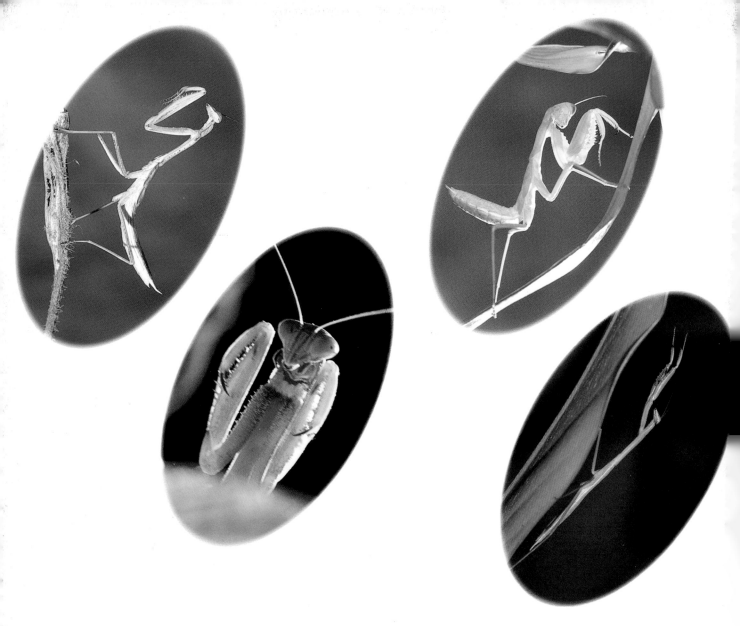

Praying Mantises

Mantises are also called praying mantises. This nickname comes from how a mantis holds its front pair of legs. It often folds them in a way that looks as though it is praying.

Its color, body shape, and pose make a mantis hard to see on a leaf or branch. When a tasty insect comes close, the mantis is waiting to strike. A mantis can snatch an insect in its front legs faster than the blink of an eye!

Food

Mantises only eat things that are alive. They are excellent hunters. They mainly eat insects. Large mantises will also eat hummingbirds, as well as small tree frogs and lizards.

A mantis uses its keen eyesight and sensitive antennae to know just when to grab a nearby insect.

A mantis has strong front legs with spiny hooks. It grasps the insect with its front legs and holds the wriggling body tight. Then it crunches up its meal with its strong mouthparts.

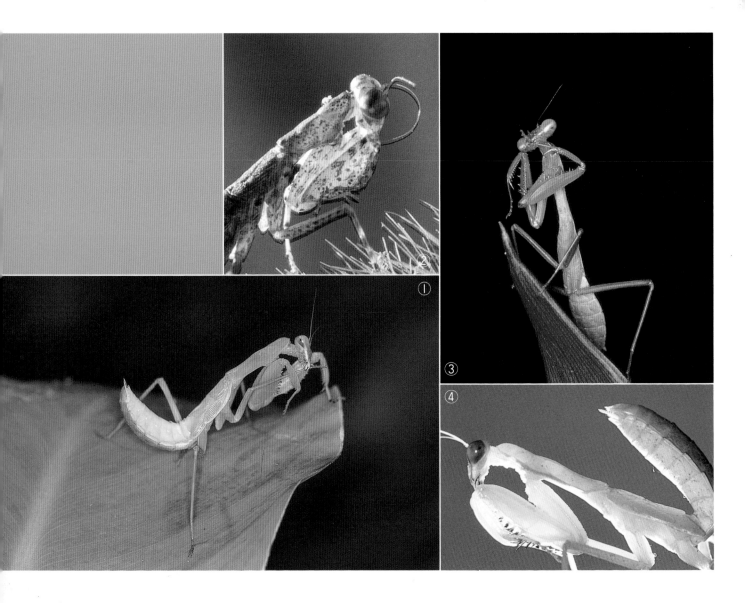

Cleaning

When a mantis finishes eating, it is time to wash up! Mantises take a lot of time and care cleaning their bodies. First, they lick their front legs. Then, almost like a cat does, they use their front legs to clean all over their heads. They even make sure their antennae are spotless!

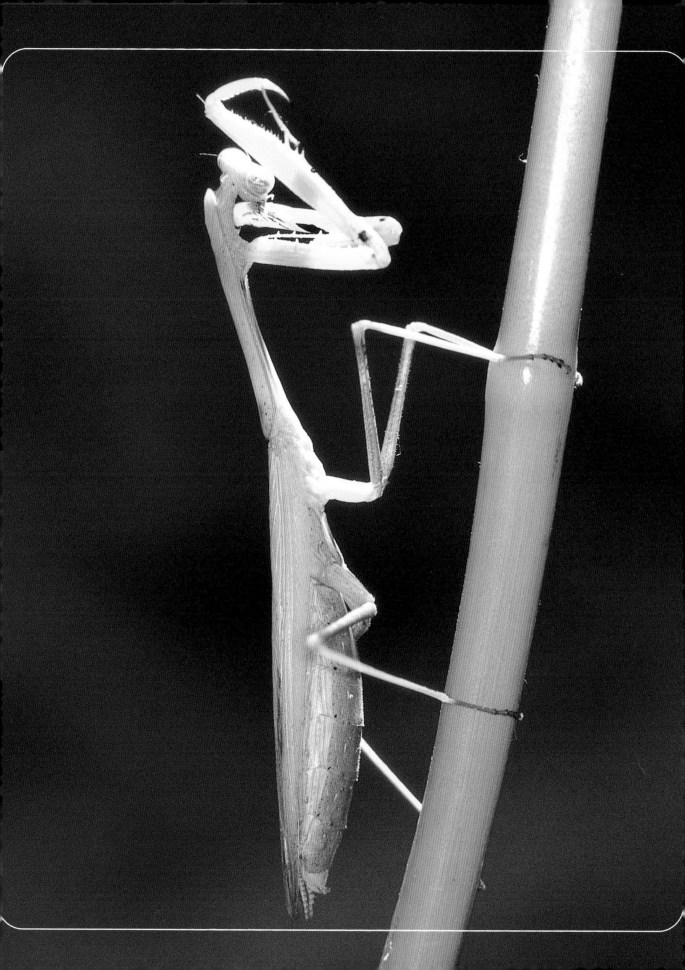

Mating

Mantises usually mate in the late summer when the female's abdomen is full of eggs. After mating, the male jumps away from the female as fast as it can. That is because the female will eat him—headfirst— if he doesn't escape!

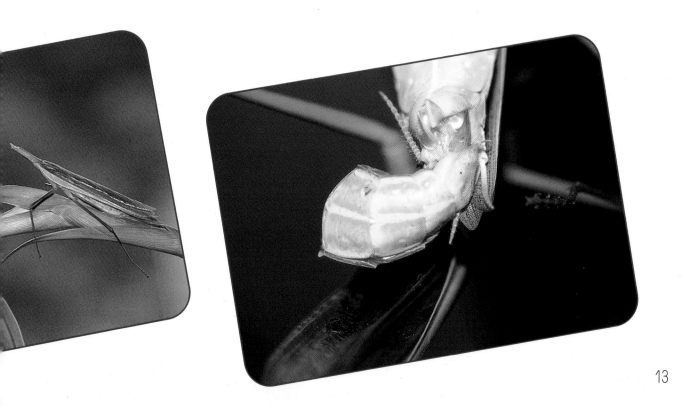

Eggs

A few days after mating, a female mantis usually finds a spot on a branch or stem to lay her eggs. Her body clings to the branch upside-down. In about 3 hours, she deposits 100 to 300 eggs within a mass of foam. The foam quickly hardens to form an egg case. This case protects the eggs through the winter as they develop inside.

Egg Cases

The inside of an egg case   An egg case in the nook of a tree.

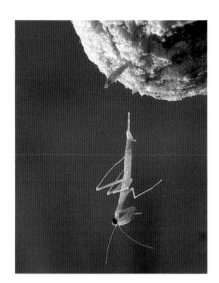

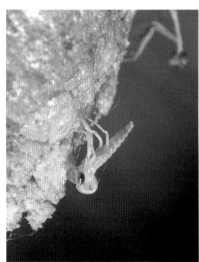

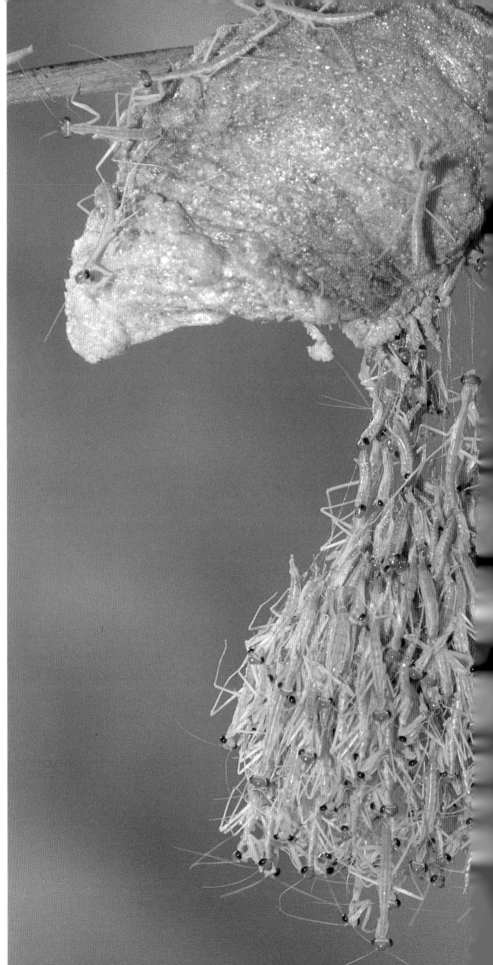

Babies

Baby mantises are called nymphs. In the spring, nymphs are ready to come out of their egg case. Hundreds of small nymphs crawl out headfirst in search of food. Their wings are too short for flying. But they reach the ground safely with the help of thin silk threads that connect each nymph to the egg case.

While they are young, nymphs are in danger of being eaten by birds, frogs, and lizards. Their pale creamy color makes them much easier to see than adult mantises. As they get older, their color darkens.

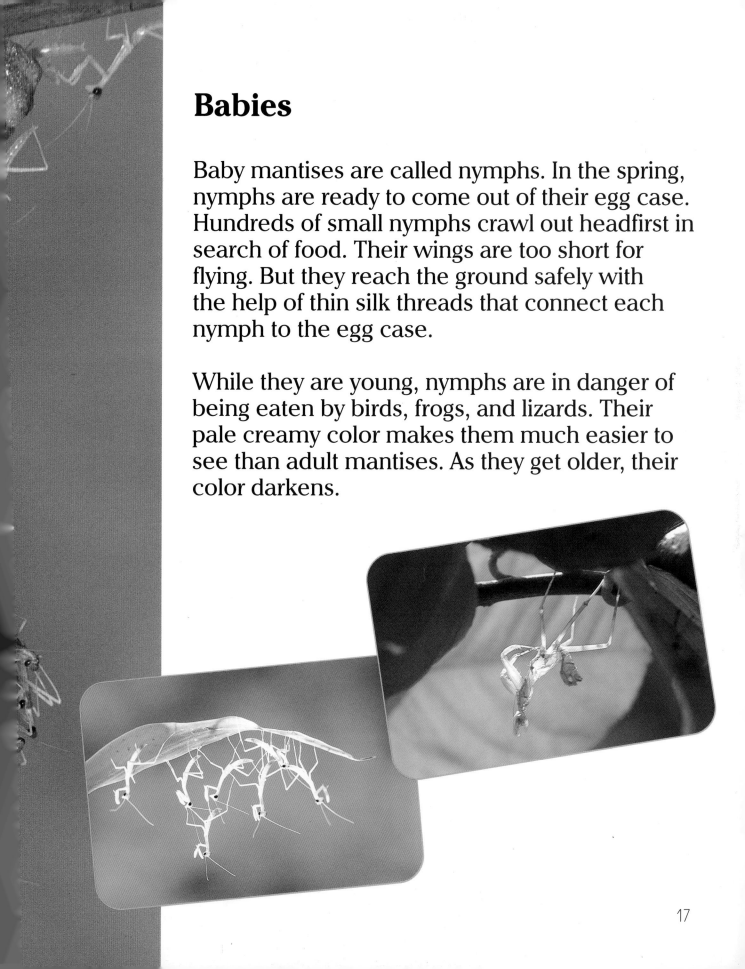

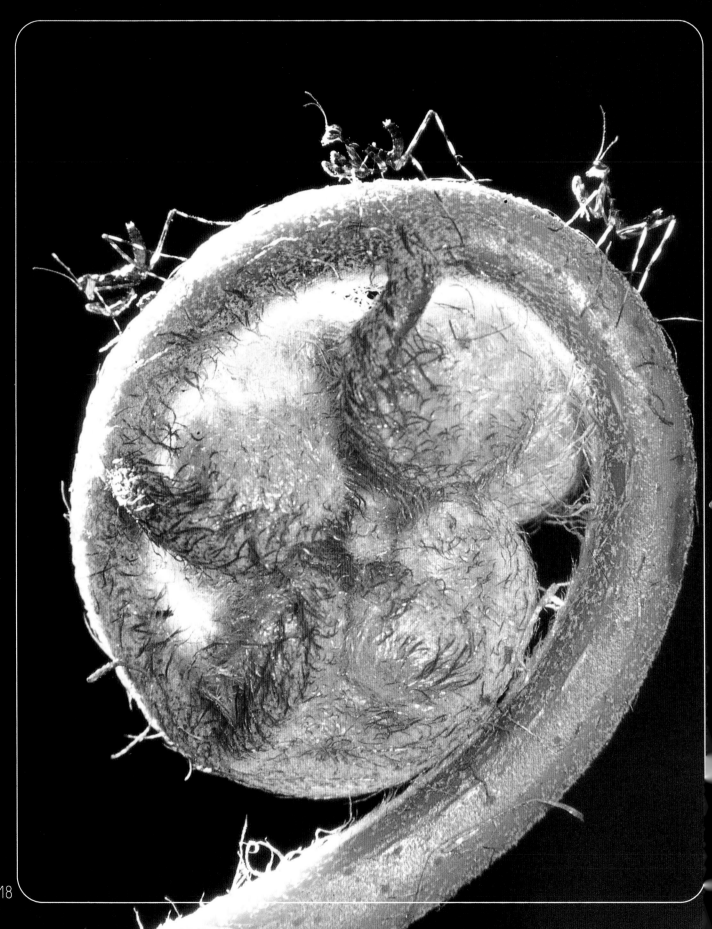

Growing Up

Insects have a hard covering over their bodies called an exoskeleton. This covering does not get bigger as an insect grows. In order to grow to its adult size, an insect has to shed its covering. This is called molting.

Nymphs molt six or seven times before they are full-grown. Each time they molt, their wings grow. The mantis also begins to change into the color it will be as an adult.

Predators

Many kinds of animals eat praying mantises. Eggs inside an egg case can be in danger from a certain kind of wasp. Ants, lizards, spiders, toads, and birds all like to eat nymphs. Nymphs will also eat each other to survive.

Birds, lizards, bats, and mice also hunt adult mantises. A mantis will spread its wings to try and scare off an attacker. It can also fly a short distance to escape.

Sometimes, a mantis gets caught in a sticky web and ends up as a meal for a spider!

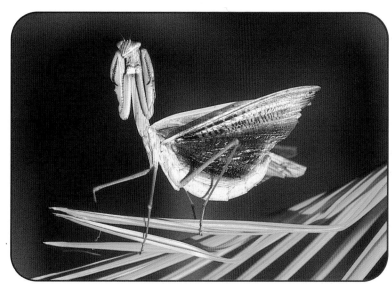

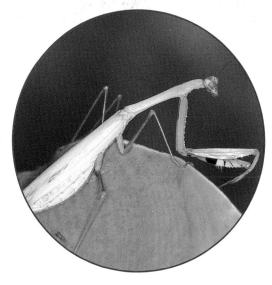

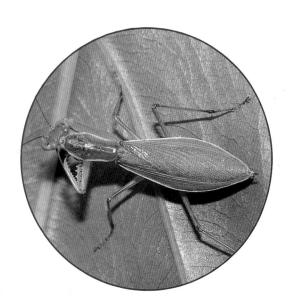

Mantises of the World

There are more than 1,500 different kinds of mantises all over the world. Some are less than 1 inch long. Others are longer than 6 inches. Mantises help people by eating bugs that hurt farm crops and garden plants. These interesting insects are an important part of our natural world.

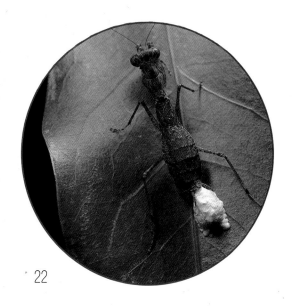

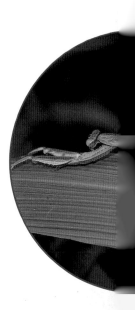

For More Information

Brimner, Larry Dane. *Praying Mantises.* Danbury, CT: Childrens Press 1999.

Johnson, Sylvia A. *Mantises.* Minneapolis, MN: Lerner, 1984.

Stefoff, Rebecca. *Praying Mantis.* New York: Marshall Cavendish, 1997.

Glossary

compound eye an eye that has many lenses

exoskeleton the hard covering on the outside of an insect's body

molt to shed the outer skin or covering

nymph a baby mantis

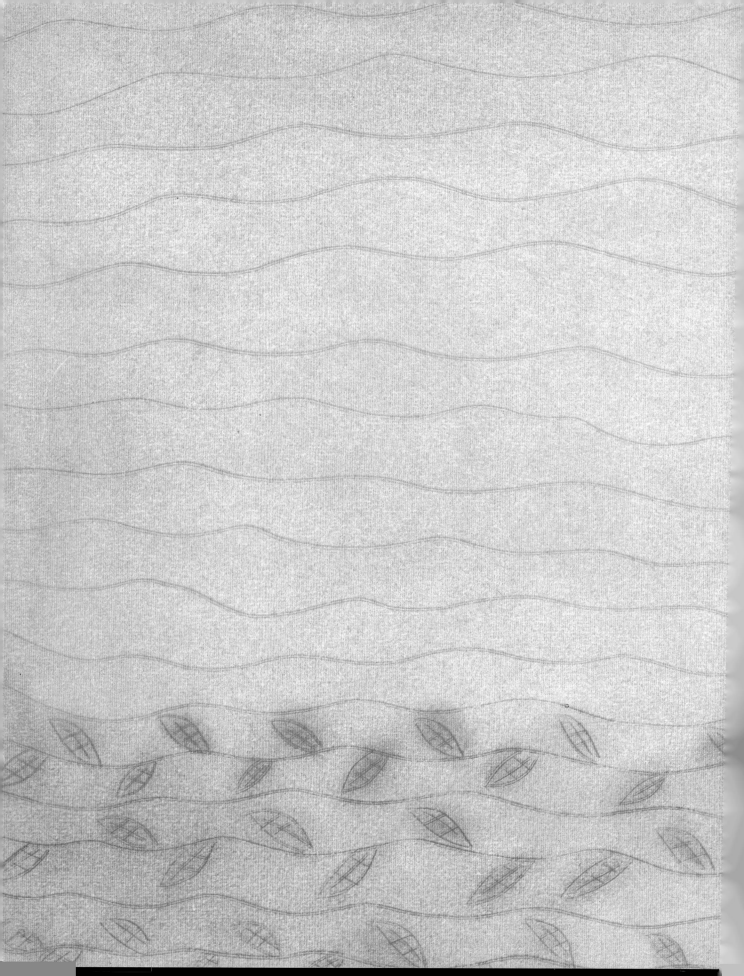